MW00412297

I CAN'T LOSE MY MIND, BECAUSE I HAVE TO FEED MY DOG

K. CLEARY

Copyright © by K. Cleary

All rights reserved. This book or any portion thereof
may not be reproduced or used in any manner
whatsoever without the express written permission
of the publisher except for the use of brief quotations
in a book review.

First Printing, 2019

ISBN: 9781089555834
Imprint: Independently published

Instagram: @k.cleary.f

Book design by Taylor Wichrowski
taylorwichrowski.com

DEDICATION

To the God who exhumed me,
the friends who sat shoulder to shoulder with me,
the sister who leaned her forehead against mine,
and the dog that said nothing and everything
in impossible times
by laying her head in my lap.

CONTENTS

BLACK

Some days I sit cross-legged
and I look down
at my open hands in my lap.
I whisper to myself,
"I am here. I am here."
Then I put my hand
to my chest
and feel my heart beat
and I realize that
it takes more than a heartbeat
to be alive.

As it turns out
I'm quite comfortable
with insanity,
knowing I'm
a little crazy.
I am quite uncomfortable
and intolerant
of hopelessness.

In regards to hope:
I pray it never leave you.
There are many things
we can live without.
Hope is not one of them.
A human without hope
is a home without people.
I will, that should it ever
become unbearable,
you use your last bit of strength
to open up your mouth
and tell somebody.

I get why many of
the great artists
did their best work in pain.
It's like you can't tell
the most honest truth,
without opening a vein.

I recognize and can occupy
the lightest lights,
because I've been through
the darkest darks.
Don't mistake my joy
for inexperience.

They say the term heartbreak
is a metaphor.
I beg to differ.
Then what is this thing
in my chest,
that feels like
it has lived
a thousand lifetimes?

Sometimes metaphors
stop being enough,
and you just have
to tell the truth.

I have been ignoring my body
for my entire life.
Never paying attention
to my heart rate,
my aches,
my breathing,
my tension,
my bouncing knee,
my tired feet.
Even good things.
No matter how safe it kept me,
I cannot divorce my body
and be fully alive.
I need it, it needs me.
It does those things for a reason,
I must listen to its plea.

Trauma is a mental photo album,
with photos
that we did not
give permission to be taken,
or saved into our memory.

Sometimes, I feel like
I am unraveling.
I look around
and I don't see any way
of knitting myself back together.
So I gather my limbs
and I hug them to my chest.
I let my mind get quiet
until I can remember
who I am,
what I've done,
and where I've come from.
And I scoop myself up
and go on.

No matter how deep the pit,
please believe
there will always
be a hand
long enough,
strong enough,
to reach you.
To pull you out.

As I lay awake
staring at the ceiling
I pray to God,
"What is this thing
in my chest,
and how does it feel
so full
and so empty
at the same time?"

Numb
is never numb.
It just means
there is too much.
There is so much.
I am so full of
things I cannot say,
of expressions
I cannot compose,
of screams I do not
have the power
to utter.

There are so many parts of myself
that I have never let meet.
So I finally resolved to do so.
I let Grief and Unfairness meet.
At first, they were at odds
refusing to speak to each other.
I returned to hear Grief say,
"you're me boiled down".
I did the same with Silence and Powerlessness,
they fell into each other
and they wailed foreheads touching.
I also introduced Rejection and Defensiveness.
They rolled their eyes at each other at first,
but when they finally made eye contact
they realized they had known each other forever
from opposite sides of a door.
I introduced Bitterness and Hope deferred.
Bitterness looked at Hope deferred
and realized it was looking
at itself in the mirror from years before.

I introduced Kindness to Hurt.
Hurt realized what it could become,
what it would become, with love.
I let Trauma meet Stop
and they walked away
hand in hand saying nothing.
I introduced these seemingly isolated pairs
and I introduced healing.
What parts of you
are you withholding from yourself?

If you promise to make space
for my brokenness,
I will promise to tell you
when I feel like
I am disappearing into it.

I promise to never shut up
about the things that matter to me
about the things that are part of me
ever again.
I will never let
all the things I don't say
become prison bars.

It's been really hard
to feel beautiful
on the inside,
with all of this
sadness in here.

Trust me.
The hurt from the healing
has been worth every tear,
every head-hold.
It pales in comparison
to the years I would lose
if I didn't give my hurt
the attention it needs.
So I will hug my hurt
while I am still young,
before it becomes an old woman
full of, "I should have's".

You are not in this head
in this heart
or in this body.
Please do not say to me,
"I know exactly how you feel."
If you do,
I shall know for sure,
that you are
not seeing me.
You are seeing you.

Do we call the clouds
weak for raining?
No. This is natural.
Needed to nourish,
to grow.
How silly we are
for believing
it is weak to weep.

I wonder
how much of my energy,
how much of my heart,
how much of my mind
I expend
trying to stay sane.
And what I could do with them
if I didn't.

This will sound harsh.
But you know,
sometimes I want
people to stay
as far away from me
as the ocean is wide.
But I also don't want to be alone.
Does that make sense?
This room is so dark and heavy.
I don't want anyone to come in.
I just want someone I love
to hold a candle
through the door frame.
Just their hand in the room
while they stand outside,
because I really need help
making light right now.

For me,
shame made it so that
I didn't even believe myself.
Even when in my gut,
I knew the truth.
It is possible
that guilt and shame
can manipulate a memory.

Recently, I find myself
holding my shoulders.
Thanking them
for all that they've held,
all that they've weathered.
Touching the skin
and kneading the muscles
that have done so much.
Telling them, "Thank you.
It's time to rest.
I'll take it from here."

In coming to meet my anger,
I am realizing that it is actually
sadness and fear and powerlessness
on fire.
Desperately reaching for
some control and agency.
Reaching for some
productivity for the pain.

Every time
I didn't say stop
I didn't say help
I didn't cry
I didn't express anger
when I needed to,
it has translated to
extra hours
I need to spend
in the classroom of myself
learning how to
tend and care for
that version of me
that I didn't get to care for
the first time.
My suppression
was me oppressing myself.

The lie.
The cage.
The gut-punch.
The hands
 tightening around my neck.
The elephant sitting on my chest.
All from the thought,
 "It is always going to be this way."

So much noise.
My hands shook
as I covered my ears
and tucked my head
between my knees
and rocked
like I knew
crazy people did.
And that was the first day
of many
that I was half-there.

I have found
that there are
some kinds of tired
that sleep cannot remedy.
In this kind of weariness
I need lots of tea.
I need to sit in the shower.
I need to hear Cat Stevens in my car.
I need dark humor.
I need to stare at the ceiling.
I need to not be fed clichés
from a conveyor belt.
I need wind and literature.
It's like instead of my eyes,
I need to close my soul
down for a while.

Cycles:
When I look at you
I wish I could see
the hurt child
I'm sure you once were.
Now I just see
you being
who I'm sure
you once hated.

When I think about
having to see your face,
hear your voice,
feel your eyes—
I cringe.
A tea kettle whistles
and screams
and pours smoke
in my head.

In spite of you.
That's what I would have said
all of this is for, months ago.
But it's not now,
it's about me.
If it's in spite of you
we are still playing
tug-of-war
over my power.
You've already taken enough,
you don't get to
have my power too.

I wish people
were like buildings
and we could put
signs up for ourselves like,
"under construction".
So people would know
we're still in progress.

Dear warrior,
Let me look at your face.
Let me see the shadows of tear stains
on your cheeks.
Let me see the chest you hold high
and the neck you lift
despite all it takes to carry around
your weary mind.
Let me see the tattered, calloused feet
you have continued to carry your body around with.
Let me touch those hands
that have been as tight as fists
and as light as leaves in the breeze.
Let me know those eyes
that have known both devastation
and restoration.
When you laugh
I can see how you have
ground your back teeth in angst.
Those knees know running
and standing firm.
All those to's and fro's,
you mortal human person,
tell your gorgeous narrative.
To let me see them,
is the ultimate gift.

I find myself wishing
there was a way
for someone to hold me
without touching me.
I think this is what
unconditional love is.

More often than not,
when I am trying to fall asleep,
the moment my head hits the pillow
thoughts creep up on me
like monsters in the dark.
A familiar record player cues up.
Track 1: All the things I need to do
Track 2: Arguments of past and future on a loop
Track 3: Shameful thoughts about what I've done
Track 4: Fear of not falling asleep which perpetuates not
falling asleep
Track 5: Things I try to forget
Shakes head, flip the record.
Track 6: Words I cannot unhear
Track 7: Friends I need to reconnect with
Track 8: About my body
Track 9: Who is disappointed in me
Track 10: Turn over and pull the covers over my head.
Who could possibly sleep with all that racket?

Trust me when I say
hate does something to the soul.
It is weed killer
in a flower bed.
Why are you letting
other people decide
about your soul things?
Let it go,
and it will let you go.

Why do we say,
"It's okay"
when it's not?
Why do we say,
"It's fine"
when it's not?
We say it before
we've even thought about
how we are.
Why is it
so damn hard
to accept help,
to tell the truth
about feeling weak
and needing someone?

Emotional things manifest
themselves physically.
Depression doesn't leave
the body alone.
Anxiety doesn't only
exist in the mind.
In your body,
anxiety can feel like you're dying
depression can feel like you're dead.
You and me need to
take some time
to make peace for and with our bodies.

I spent so much time
trying to beat my emotions.
Like they were a level of a game
that I got stuck on.
But there was no mystery to solve,
no problem to quantify,
no hidden metaphor.
They just needed to be felt.

I have made an identity
out of guilt.
My conscience
works overtime.
But I only get paid
in racing thoughts,
in hours of sleep lost.

I'll just quietly whisper to myself,
"I am enough."
And as I hear it
rattle off of my lips,
I'll try to forget
that I am faking.
And I'll try to believe it.
I'll try to say it
again
and again,
until I know it's true
and I don't have to say it
to myself
with a stream of hot, salty water
running down my face
hitting my bedroom sheets.

There are many
different kinds of tears.
Some for grief.
These are like steady rain
down your face.
Some for silence.
These ones are loud
and they often fight their way out.
Some for fear.
These ones involve trembling
and a galloping heart rate.
Some for anger.
These ones contort the face.
I hope whichever
your last ones were,
your tears water you
so you can bloom.

My love,
if something that happened
quite a long time ago,
upon thought,
still brings about
very fresh tears
or a racing heart
or a quivering lip,
it needs attention.
It needs tending to.
Don't allow it
to continue
to go unloved.

The pain of trauma
is in the details.
Please remember
they live with us every day.
In triggers,
in feelings,
in sounds,
in smells,
in memories,
in familiarity.

We will continue
to pour ourselves out
no container beneath,
until we make
our own peace
a priority.

Sometimes I make it
through a whole day
without taking
a single deep breath.
Do you do this?
Unconsciously live
with shallow breath?

A 3:00 am prayer:
Please let me know
for certain,
let me hear from you,
let me feel that,
"It is going to be okay.
It will pass.
Just breathe."

It takes wisdom to know
when to whisper
and to know
when to roar.

Sometimes when I weep
I can feel the tears
of past generations
of my family
running down my face,
running out of my eyes.
Because previous eyes
held them in
and folded them
inside themselves,
afraid they would splash others.

I hope that I can learn
to love despite my wounds,
instead of loving out of them.
I hope I can stop
seeing you as a target
when I'm frightened.

When your legs are sore
they'll ask you
what you did yesterday.
If you worked out.
If you slept wrong.
If you walked a far distance.
When your heart is sore,
they rarely ask about
what happened yesterday.

When I am very sad
I feel like I am an imposter
in joyful spaces,
around joyful people.
So I take several steps back
out of the room
that I wasn't in
in the first place.
Depression thrives
on a diet of isolation.
I'm trying to know better.

He asked me how I was
and I said, "You know,
all drama aside
I feel like I am sitting
in a room
that is on fire
and I am just sitting there
in the blaze
being consumed
not doing anything about it,
just thinking,
well this is this."

I've learned that
sometimes
I force rejection
so that I don't have to face it
at the hands
of someone else.

Trauma's worst enemy
is power.
Because when it happened
we didn't have a say.
Now we need to say
what we couldn't say
so that the power
can talk back
to the trauma
and tell it
it is not
the only voice
in our lives.

A caution:
There is a way to hide
inside of yourself.
While it seems wise
and safe at first,
it becomes hard for
people to find you
even when they're looking
right at you.

Sometimes it's like
my strength and my power
are playing hide and seek from me,
and I'm just left
searching for them
with a body that has a memory
but doesn't know
what to do with itself.

I have always found healing
by telling my story.
But the thing about trauma
is that many times
there is not a story to tell
or at least not
a comprehensive one.
It is as if you dropped
a glass of water,
and you have hundreds
of shards of glass,
each a small part of the whole
but impossible to make sense of.
It's fragmented and sharp
and very difficult
to put back together.

Stitches vs. A Band-Aid:
Healing through things
rather than healing over things.
One is easier,
but it is also less permanent.
One is much more painful,
but it stays.

The 6th sense of a woman:
I believe there is some sort of
extra sense engrained into women.
I don't think we are born with it;
I think we learn it.
Which is even more sad.
I know it sounds crazy.
I get this sense around certain people,
it is usually certain men.
Don't call us dramatic.
Too many of our sisters, ourselves,
have experienced what
has made this sense necessary.
I can feel my heart beat fast
and my skin get hot
while I fight to remain stone-faced
on the outside.
I try to conceal my eyes
scanning the room for an exit.

Like an animals' ears perk up
when it senses danger
we can sense the threat.
We have adapted a sense
to feel your eyes
to know what kind
of looking you're doing.
We have adapted a sense
to know how close you are
without looking at you.
Even the very idea of
this adaptation hurts,
and it does not always keep
the danger away.

And I'll pray to God,
I'll ask for
a heightened awareness
of good, of hope, of joy
even when the actual portion
within myself
cannot be big.

Numbness will not listen
to your preferences.
It will not take the time
to sort good from bad.
It will take it all.
I now keep this in mind
when I want to shut up
and shut down.

Words on my mind the most lately,
essential to my progress, my process:

Toxic Masculinity
Trauma
Gas-Lighting
Shame
Micro-Aggression
Privilege
I believe you
Cultural Humility
Invalidation
Me too
Mutual Benefit

Hype Women
Conversational Narcissism
Attachment
Spiritual Bypassing
Dissociation
Echo Chambers
Radical Self-Acceptance
and love and love and love.

These are showing me
both how far I've come
and how much farther
I need to go.

I am afraid to go back
and read my old journals.
There are so many of them.
And then I remember
that I didn't imprison my pain.
I held it, I felt it, and set it free.
So I don't have to worry about
it escaping from the pages
and returning to me.

Do not fool yourself.
I used to believe that
a mastery of
psychological self-control,
not crying,
was pure strength.
I have slowly
and saltily
come to realize
that each tear
that charges down the cheek
is an admission of humanness
of feeling
of true, authentic,
beautiful, vulnerable
strength.

We must all
learn the difference
between sharing
a similar experience
and knowing
how someone else feels.
This is an
essential lesson
and the difference
between seeing someone,
and missing them entirely.

Tell me more about this thing
called the friend zone.
How it is such a curse
to be my friend
when you feel like
you have a right
to my body.
In the future,
you should know that
if she has let you be her friend
she may be sharing more intimacy
with you anyways.

At birth,
we are born with
the instinctive ability
to breathe.
And somewhere along the way
a lot of us forgot how.
So we must relearn,
reteach ourselves how.

When I came down
from my birds-eye view
and began participating
in my own life,
that is when I knew
I was beginning to heal.

In an attempt
to bring empathy
to men for women
we have found
creative ways like,
what if she was
your mother
your sister
your daughter.
If we began using
the unmediated truth—
what if she was human,
or your equal?
Would we still
need creative ways,
to help men feel?

Sometimes I think that
I will never be happy
with this body.
I fear for the years ahead
as I grieve for the years behind
of it saying longingly,
"Please, love me, be kind to me."
I say to it in words, looks, and thoughts,
"Healthy isn't enough, you must be perfect."
So I say to myself,
"Okay, that's the next journey."

You demanded I stand up
when you constantly
swept the rug out from under me.
It was a bruised and tiring way
for a girl to grow.

The sadder I get
the more I bleed poetry.

A lie:
You are made not normal
or deficient
because of your trauma.
The truth:
Your response is actually
the normal thing,
and the experience was
the not normal thing.
Your response
whatever it may be
is actually remarkable,
it's you keeping yourself alive.

Pity, sympathy, empathy.

Pity is, "Sorry. It won't get better.

Hi down there."

Sympathy is, "I'm sorry for you,

but I have to go."

Empathy is, "That looks hard,

mind if I sit down?"

People will remember the difference.

I know I do.

She asked me why I write.
I closed my eyes and smiled
and said, "How could I not
share my survival guide?"

Your trauma,
after a while
the choice to address it
comes down to ownership.
Do you own you?
Or does your trauma own you?
If it's the latter
I hope you have hope.
I hope you know
that it can be different.

I wish I could have been
the cork on your liquor bottle.
I would have refused to move.

Depression
is going to wish
it never showed
its sorry face
up to the doorstep
of my heart.
I don't know all of them,
but I know many
of its secrets.
The way it
chokes the soul
like a weed.
And you can bet
I'm going to out
every single one of them
to anyone who will listen.

Please do not shush me.
Often, to shush is to shame.
If you do, then you are either
saying you are more
concerned about
how others see you
than you are about me,
or you are uncomfortable with
my vulnerability,
or you don't want to hear
what I have to say.
Chances are,
if I am upset to the point
of audible expression,
there is a reason.
Shame is not a cherry,
please do not put it on top.

I have found that
when I am low
I don't believe my own,
"Things are going to be okay",
and so I need to ask
a friend to borrow theirs.

Do you ever feel like
you've lent out your exhale?
And find yourself only inhaling?
I feel like I become
so full with each compromise,
each pang of guilt,
each time I pour
from an empty place,
each time I have to
re-establish boundaries,
each time I have to
explain myself.
My face gets a darker
shade of purple.
And I need to be allowed
to exhale.

On Therapy:
I asked for this.
I asked to be disassembled
and wiped clean.
You cannot protect yourself
for a lifetime
and then expect
vulnerability,
emotions,
health,
to feel easy.
Pleasant.
Still, I know
this is important.
Reassembly is painful,
but it is also
paving the way
for the rest of my life.

I am amazed at
how many layers of skin I have,
how many layers of strength,
how many times
I am sure I won't get through.
How much my skin
is shed or torn or stretched,
and then still
I realize a new layer of strength.

I used to think
that I couldn't feel anything.
That I was numb,
confused at least.
I was wrong.
I just got used to feeling
everything at once,
all the time.
And it didn't kill me.
It didn't kill me.
Now I know how to
walk around on fire.
I know how to burn and survive.
Now that I've got the hang of it,
I'll light the way for others.

Cleave to the feeling
of sunshine on your face.
Close your eyes
and remember it.
Study it, tuck it away.
You're going to need it.

Sometimes
it is hard to remember
the sunshine
when it has been raining
for a while.

In my third month of therapy
my therapist saw my face warp
in simultaneous grief, sadness,
shame, and anger.
She said softly, "hold that space."
I had no idea what the hell that meant.
I wanted to drop that space
like it was on fire.
I think I understand now.
It means saying the things
that you thought you would never
say out loud.
It means a lot of
hellish, confusing months.
It means a mass of
memory and emotion
that you didn't know
one person could feel.
Thinking the next day
will be the day
that you collapse under it.

It means you leave therapy
not just more educated
about yourself
as I had done before,
but more than that—alive.
At home in yourself.
That's what holding space is.
It's holding the raw parts of you
out in the open for months
or maybe even years,
so that you don't have to
hold them for the rest of your life.

I never loved those quotes
that begin with "you are...".
The ones where the author
assumes to know you.
Until I found myself
in a place
where I was not
able to be comforted
by much other than
the words of strangers
who knew something about pain.
I now pay homage to those
who care to write words for people
that they do not know.

Sometimes I want to scream
"save me",
 and then I think,
"no wait, I will."

At rock bottom,
I found hope
tenderly waiting
with a trampoline.

I CAN'T LOSE MY MIND, BECAUSE I HAVE TO FEED MY DOG

GREY

For me, humility
has looked like
getting asked a question
and replying with
"I'm not sure"
to the same question
I used to have
an affirmative answer to.
I sometimes find myself wishing
that things still felt
that black and white.
But I'm finding greyness
holds mercy all the more.

Transforming thoughts into beliefs:
Treat them like a small child.
Nurture it,
speak to it kindly,
let it cry,
let it laugh,
let it explore,
let it be defiant,
allow it to fall,
and get back up,
until it finds its way.

'How far I've come' is a friend
that I look back on frequently
on hard days.
I nod at it fondly
with my hands in my pockets
as I walk on.

I want to warn you
about making sense of things.
It helps,
but it doesn't heal.
For that,
you must grieve.
And grief isn't only about death
it's about loss.
Swim through that loss
and remember to come up
for air every now and then.

I think healing
is a lesson in learning
to love yourself.
Silently thanking and stroking
the protective spirit
that kept you alive,
and sending it fondly
on its way
as wholeness
takes its place.

My triggers are single strings
poking out of a mass
of threads that I've woven
over a lifetime
to keep me together,
to keep me alive.
Backs and forths
unders and overs and knots.
Someone pulls on one string
and a big piece of
what holds me together unravels.
My overreactions
are usually the result
of pulling on threads
of old wounds.

The world taught me
not to feel.
So I go to my books,
so I go to my songs,
so I walk around
when the sun gets golden,
so I go to the films
that make me weep.
All to remember
the way I started
before the world
had its say.
All this time thinking
I was moving forward
not feeling,
now trying
to find my way back.

We will pass sadness
anger, use,
abuse, unkindness,
and pain
to our future children
and their families.
These things will
run thick through generations
until someone is ready
to feel them
to heal them
and then throw them
in the trash
instead of recycle them.

I think that when people say
you are not what happened to you,
they are wrong.
Because in so many ways
we are strong
we are kind
we are compassionate
we are deep
because our experiences made us so.
So we should revise it to
we are not JUST
what happened to us.
Because we are what happened to us
in a good way
and so much more.

Since I was a little girl
there has always been
this small anger inside of me.
It flushed through my cheeks
and made the hair on my arms
stand on end.
I felt it in my lungs as they
forced air in and out.
I felt it in my stomach
when wrong and bad things
happened to people
and no one did anything about it.
It came up studying history in school.
I looked around to see if
anyone else felt it.

It came when people made
offensive jokes
and when people
spoke untruths.
It came when I saw
hateful people
get ahold of a microphone.
When someone made
the people I love
weep, or yell, or cower.
It has taken years to understand
that this anger is justice.
And it's a good thing.

Why do we disable our power
when others say we are strong
by saying, "I didn't have a choice".
Yes we did.
Own your power.
Own your resilience.
Your arrival to the
current conversation
shows you made a choice.
You are not still there
trying to decide
whether or not to stand firm.
You are here.

When you are caught in the lie
that loving yourself
is pride, or vanity, or egotistical
a confident person
who loves herself
feels like a threat.
It feels like,
"Who do you think you are?
How dare you love yourself, if I can't."

When you have to search
through gritted teeth
or a raised heart rate
for an "I love you",
perhaps the other person
does not deserve to hear it.
And that's alright.
Your "I love you's"
are not cheap,
don't hand them out
to just anyone.

The dearest kind of friend
will sit with you
when rivers fall down your face,
or when you are so sad
your tears are dry.
She will just softly
fold her hand into yours
and stare ahead with you
letting you know
she is there
for all that is to come.
That kind of friend
does not even need
to open their mouth
to love you.

One of the first rhymes
I learned as a child
was the sticks and stones one.
I will never teach
my future children this lie.
I remember words
from 6-years-old.
I still hear them.
I will teach my children
the power of words
so that they will use them
and know their power.
So that they will know
that they are allowed
to feel broken over them.
So that they will not take up
sticks, or stones, or words as weapons.

118

Ownership
Dominate
Possess
Rule
Entitlement
Property
Use
Mine.
These are words
you can say
about household items.
Not about me.
Not about my sisters.
Not about any human.

For me,
trust has never been a bone
grown strong and sturdy.
It is more like a muscle
that needs to be worked out
and kneaded with tender care.

I do not want to be bound
by the side of the bed
I woke up on.
I want to have the choice
to put my feet on the ground
on the side
where the sun
peaks through the shades.
The side of hope.

I have been trying
to train my heart
to re-educate it
to expect
kindness and affection
from men
instead of rejection and hurt.
Might it set me up
for more hurt? Sure.
But it will also allow me
to accept the good
should it come along.

It's been a lifetime
since I've had someone
crawl on top of me,
the only intimacy in mind
to look at me right in the eyes.

Sometimes I feel guilty for
needing a reason
not to do something.
Declining someone
when I don't have the time or space
to offer them.
Then I remind myself,
at least now I can say no.
Even if I still feel
like I need a reason.
Where I used to say yes anyways.
Sometimes growth
is a small voice saying,
"each small step is a big step".

Can I be honest with you?
Sometimes a poem sits
written for days
trapped in my head
or my phone notes
or my notebook
until my brave
gets big enough
to show her to you.

It's really frightening
to want things.
To throw your "can I's"
into the universe
hoping beyond hope
that they come back
with a "yes".
It is hard to be disappointed
when you haven't invested
some serious want.

He turned to me
and asked what it was like
on lonely nights.
And I told him.
And he said
he was thinking of me
on all of those nights too.
That he would pray
and ask God that,
"she would learn to love herself
before she loves me
so that when the time came
she could love me
and know that she
was worthy of love too."

Dear pride,
I know that
your fundamental purpose
is to protect my dignity,
but I want you to know
that I am henceforth
giving the ones closest to me
permission to
lift a mirror to you
when you get too big
and reveal that you
are actually
insecurity in armor.

Whatever stands in the way
of your peace.
No matter how romantic
no matter how sparkly
no matter how deep you're in it,
it needs to go.

Ever made eye contact with someone,
enough to study the glassy surface
without wavering?
Did it make you
feel like crying?
Extraordinarily exposed?
There is something to this.
It is equally relieving
and frightening
to have someone
see into you
when you are not used to it.

It took me some time to realize
that just because
someone says
you are wrong or bad
doesn't mean you are.
It's okay to give yourself
the loving permission
to question the legitimacy
of what people say to you.

I am just trying
to learn to be
a consistent person.
The same me in
all my spaces
in all my days.
Not bending or shifting
based on who I am around
or what mood I am in
or where I am
to impress or compete.
Being unedited
is taking my identity back
from resting in
the hands of others.

Remember the times
when you threw
your hopes and dreams
up into the sky
and hoped they
would become stars?
Use those constellations
to give you hope now
while you're in the trenches
making new stars.

As children we forget
that our moms and dads
had lives and stories
before they were
moms and dads.
They had hopes
and dreams
and pains
and failures
and adventures
and heartbreak.
We must remember this
when they are not perfect,
when we pluck them out of context
and expect them to be flawless.

There are thousands of words
that I wish I could lasso
and pull back out of the air.
I think about things I've said
and I am so sorry for them.
My only offering
at the feet of their receivers
is the promise to do better.

I'm learning that as I get
deeper with God,
that prayer looks less like
folded hands
eyes closed
bowed head
neat life.
And more like
knees to floor
whispers in the quiet
tears to cheek
chuckles and eyes up
and deep worshipful breaths.

For a while,
I used to throw
my story in full
at new people in my life.
Almost trying to hedge
any possibility
of being misunderstood.
Like I owed it to them
to explain why I am the way I am.
Now I have learned
that my story
your story
any story,
is a privilege
that not everyone has earned.
And if I am misunderstood
it is not because
I do not know who I am,
it is because
they do not know who I am.

I will not allow the lie
that I can only write
meaningful things
from a place of pain
become a reality.
While there is meaning
and growth
and acceptance
and depth in pain,
it is not art
to keep pain around.
I do not want it
to be my legacy.

I have realized
that regret can run
as thick in the body
as any illness.
It's like the common cold
not too bad at first
but if left unattended
if you let it thrive
it can be life threatening.
The best medicine for regret
is forgiving yourself
for the choices you made
and coughing out the
"should have's" and the
"could have's"
until the "I am's" heal you.

I look at you
and I think about
picking teams at recess.
I think about
looking at my teammates
and thinking, "we're stacked."
Every single part
of the team
is incredible.
I see you and I see
a person so worthy of love.
I wish you could
look at yourself
and see a winning team.
– for Colleen

Sometimes I feel like
I've created a self-imposed timeline,
telling me how long
I'm allowed to struggle
before it gets old to others.
As it lapses
I feel my mouth
steal an answer from my heart
bullying it to say, "doing better".
I must remind myself that
no one is watching
a clock or a calendar
looking at my healing process
and shaking their head
in disappointment.
My now people
are not my then people.

It never occurred to me
that I could just stop
pretending to know
what I was doing
and just ask for help.

In my dreams
I ask the brave version of me
how she did all those things.
She turns her head to me
thoughtfully and says,
"we don't all think in insecurities".

As a girl
I started out this
tangley, wild, wonder-filled,
dirty, strange thing.
I looked around
and I saw I was the only one.
So I slowly tamed myself,
watching others
normalizing myself
fitting in.
It's one of the worst mistakes
I have ever made.
Now I am peeling back
the layers of tameness
I have plastered to myself
to find that
tangley, wild, wonder-filled
dirty, strange thing.
And set her free.

To you who can
transform pain into beauty,
you are magic makers.
You cry out your tears of pain
into your hands
and you throw them into the sky
and they become stars
lighting up the dark night sky.

What if we measured
our strength
in emitting softness that
wasn't offered to us?

When it comes
to being a shoulder.
Avoid offering clichés.
They make somebody
feel like an anybody.
See the person in front of you,
not a problem.

Some simplification:
In this life
it is impossible to avoid harm
and it is nearly impossible
to do no harm.
It is very hard
to be a person.
It's important
to remember this
as we walk around
each day.

I am so so deeply sorry
if my desire
to maintain the status quo
has trampled on you
being seen or heard,
trampled on your justice,
trampled on your truth.

I knew and I know
that I am going to have to
draw a road map
so that when I run
probably again and again
you know where to find me,
on the swing set of my imagination
up in the tree of my mind
in the attic of my heart.

I want to be
a walking contradiction.
Solid and strong
soft and kind.
Deep as the ocean
and as light as spring rain.
Spirited and earthed
intellectual and wise.
Calm and pensive
vivid and alive.
It has taken me
26 years to learn
none of these are
mutually exclusive.
That I am allowed to be
'and' not limited to 'or'.

When I'm on my own planet
when I'm far away in the same room
I need you to look at me and say,
"Your many parts are not
a broken shattered whole,
but a complex beautiful sum
of you-ness, lovely, a treasure.
All the hurt that comes with you
is not a sacrifice I make
nor a debt that you owe me for tolerating.
I love you more for it."

I wanted things to be better
so I put a quote as my phone background,
I read self-help books
until my eyes hurt,
I listened to the podcasts,
I had post-it notes
on my mirror.
There was nothing wrong
with these things.
But they stayed separate from me
like oil and water
until I held the space, the pain,
that needed holding.
Until I could sit face to face
with myself and like it.
Sitting still without the add ons,
content with me
before the self-help make-up.

A caution:
When offering advisement
on how to walk through
mental illness,
be careful with your "justs".
There is nothing about it
that warrants the advice
"just.."
either in the format
"just do this"
"you just have to"
"just be happy"
there is nothing small
or easily conquerable enough
about it
that warrants a "just".

I have decided
not to make decisions
on sad days.
To just wave at it
as it passes
and saves my choices
for when I have
all versions of me
at the table.
When sadness,
anger, or fear
don't exclusively
have the mic or the agenda.

When my life gets fast
and privilege lies
and tells me I am entitled to things,
when its rained for days in a row,
when I am running late,
when I am down to the last $15 in my bank account,
when my dog peed on the floor
as I'm running out the door,
when traffic gets the best of me,
and there's not enough hours in the day.
I whisper and recite to myself,
"kindness costs nothing,
kindness costs nothing,
kindness costs nothing."

On some days
I am a tender
ethereal piano melody.
On others I am
the violent galloping
of a drum.
They each protect each other
in different ways.
The piano protects the drum
by maintaining
wonder and lightness.
The drum protects the piano
from getting played
and trampled on.

I would hate
to be remembered
for who I was before
I knew things,
before I knew myself.
So I try to give others
the same benefit of the doubt
and let them be
who they are now
instead of who they are
in my memory.

I wish we were as good at
detecting lies within ourselves
as we are detecting them from others.
How come when
someone else lies
it seems an obvious fallacy
but when we lie to ourselves
we need constant
perhaps years of debunking.

For me,
isolation is the
preoccupation
of dysfunction
of malfunction
and I must
seek connection
for recuperation.

What if we believed
we were always
where we needed to be,
and if it be good
then enjoy it,
and if it be bad
know it is raising us?

I think that gratitude
has a way of
crawling over ugly things.
It's hard to feel bad
with your hands open,
with your palms up.

It will surely cost you something
in this world
to be tender.
There will likely be scars
both visible
and invisible,
but no one's last words were ever,
"I wish I loved less".

I can love you
and be responsible *to* you
but I am not
responsible *for* you.
There's a difference.
There is a space
where I begin and you end,
and a space
where you begin and I end.
Boundaries do not have to be walls.
They can simply
be claiming your own skin
as your own.

I am not going to
pour myself like water
into someone's
outstretched cupped hands
who can't hold me.
I have the depth
and mystery of and ocean
inside of me.

There is a difference between
reading 'I love you' on a screen
and reading it on a piece of paper
that you know a person touched
as their pen grooved and looped.
There is a difference between
quietly resting your head
on the shoulder of a friend
and them not worrying
if your tears get on their shirt,
and receiving a meme of
the Friends theme song
'I'll be there for you'.
This pseudo connection
is causing starvation
and we are so hungry
for each other.

I've been thinking about
how much I need
the people I love right now.
How much they've
shown up for me.
And I am privileged in friends.
I don't know how
people make it through such times
without these people.
But they do.
All the time.
That hurts so much.
Let yourself feel that.
Let's pay closer attention.

An experiment:
As a woman, count how many times
you apologize for things throughout the day.
Things that don't warrant an apology.
We have been apologizing for existing
all of our lives.
So many of us aren't even aware.
It comes out automatically.
Count how many times
you hear your sister's say it.
You won't be able to unhear it.
My ears are bleeding with all
of the apologies I hear.
The need to repent for taking up space.
Let's allow ourselves
a human amount of room.

You know how those compliments
go in one ear and out the other?
It happens so fast
you blink and they're gone.
You cling to the memory of them,
but they never taste as good
in your memory.
They tasted like honey when they came
but the withdrawal tastes like vinegar.
They leave so fast
and they will never stay
until you don't need them
to love your body
to love yourself.

I don't know if you know this,
I didn't until recently,
but there is enough of everything to go around.
There is enough beauty and talent
and uniqueness and kindness
and benevolence and intelligence
and courage to go around.
Just because someone else
is something
doesn't mean you can't
also be that something too
in your own way.
Someone else's having something
doesn't detract from your something.
It adds diversity and beauty to that something
to a world sorely in need of it.
That force that compares,
is the same one
that sets us against each other.

Do you ever feel like
between sleeping and waking
between memories and dreams
it all gets a little bit confusing?

When you shut
the door of emotion
on bad and painful things
you also shut the door
on good and joyful things.
Numbness does not take
the day off for joy.

Let us clarify:
Not taking care of yourself,
giving and never asking,
not needing anything or anyone,
always saying yes,
going until you drop,
glorifying busy—
this is not selflessness
this is self-destructiveness.
Most women
have been taught
this is expected.

If I change my mind
or my opinion,
it doesn't make me bad,
or unstable,
or insecure,
or wavering.
It means I can say
I was wrong.
I can say I know better now.
I can say I am learning humility.
We are rivers.
The minute we stop changing
we stagnate,
and become swamps.

An experiment:
Go sit in a room,
pick any person.
Imagine that person
carries even ¾
of what you carry.
Watch the empathy grow.
If we were a little more
aware of what it costs
to be alive
for others too,
I think we would all
tread more gently.

I put down the feeling
of responsibility for
the people I love
a few years ago.
Every so often,
I want to pick it back up.
Then I remind myself
that anything,
any instruction
any advice
any urgings
or convictions
I put in their hands
are mine and not theirs
and thus will fall through
their fingers like sand.
They won't stay.
And so the only thing
I should be putting in their hand
is my own.

Poetry is when you read something
and you wonder how on earth
this stranger knows precisely
what I am feeling.
How healing it is
to know we are not alone.

When did our skill
for self-sabotage
surpass our capacity
for rejection?

Set a reminder in your mind
that you have done hard things before.
And you are here.
Fill up your lungs with air
release it slowly.
And remember your survival record.
Mostly, life is
challenge after challenge
after joy after joy
after lesson after lesson.
Remember the situations
that sat on your mind
telling you that
you wouldn't get through
but you did anyway.
Remember those,
and you'll get to
the peace after peace.

Whatever keeps you
awake at night
stunts your mental
and physical rest.
Try putting it to bed
by giving it
more than just
the attention
it can steal when
your mind is weary.

I never understood why
when people see a niche
they start a business,
but when people see a pain
they don't do something about it.
Maybe it's because
we often use our
love and compassion
as a currency
instead of giving it freely.

A remedy for a sad day:
a bunch of fresh daisies
a handful of your dearest friends
1 pot of homemade mac' n' cheese
6 hours of sunshine
2 miles of bike riding
1 long hug
1 tall glass of raspberry lemonade
3-5 affirmations
several prayers
3-5 long soft gusts of wind
1 book to make you laugh and cry
lavender oil and a warm bath
repeat as needed.

I must constantly whisper to myself,
"strength doesn't have to
look like hardness,
strength doesn't have to
look like hardness".

I've found that
not being affected by things
is more concerning
than being affected by things.

Have you ever
walked by a mirror
and just not looked?
Because you know
you aren't going to like
what you see,
so you avoid seeing yourself
altogether?

Other people's pain
is not a good measuring stick
for the validity and experience of your own.
It all matters.
Does it serve anything
other than your opinion
of your humility,
to forget about what was hard?

Compartmentalizing
is a beautiful thing
when you are broken.
You can be
the healthy part of you
for a time.
It can also be a curse
because you can lose
the wholeness of who you are
in separate boxes that you've packed away.
Pack away your pain
and it gets cut off from
the love it needs to heal.

We have about as much potential
as a box of matches.
For good or bad.
We can be a source
of heat and light
or we can be an ignition
a catalyst of damage.

I used to think that
the vines, roots, and brambles
of my family tree
were wrapping around me
tightening around my throat,
my legs, and my hands.
Once I stopped trying
to rip them off of me,
I could apprehensively
climb up into the branches
and realize I am part of something
that has both good and bad,
something that sits behind me
like a landscape in a painting
and without it, I don't make sense.
I realized that if I stayed long enough
I may see it grow fruit again.

I spent so much
time and effort
into not being
whatever wound
they said I was:
unintelligent
unworthy
not enough
unattractive
harsh.
I came upon a point
where I realized
my identity was more about
who I was trying not to be
than who I was.
Outrunning wounds
instead of just being me.

I finally sat down quietly
and I checked in with myself
to make sure
it was true healing
and not just
busyness and distraction.
To ensure that
it was really peace,
and not wellness
manufactured by
my desire for closure.

WHITE

Light, I missed you.
I'm sorry I thought
it was you who had left
when I was really
covering my own eyes.

After the relief
comes the wisdom
and the sight to see
how these things
have affected you.
You look back
and in your words,
in your actions,
you recognize
traces of your wounds.
How much they creep
into your relationships
your daily conversations
your decisions
and you may
have to mourn that.

I may need some time in becoming,
but today is the first day
I've been excited about tomorrow
in a long time.
I think it's called hope.
I feel like I am slowly
returning to myself.
It's not an arrival
but it's a start.

There is no
convenient time to heal.
It's always excruciating.
Like the resetting of bones.
But you'll breathe
for the first time.
The kind of breath
you didn't know you could have.
You didn't know existed.
And eventually
you will find yourself
wondering how life
could be so lovely.

If it's good
then it's good.
If there's joy
then there's joy.
Dear overthinker
don't worry about the why.

I think that
for some things
there is no "healed"
there is only "healing"
and that is okay.
That is okay.

All I can say
is that I don't need
a big house,
only a corner to read in
and sit in the sun.
I don't need my name on anything
other than the hearts
of the people
that I love.

On admitting to humanness:
Once I started getting good
at being wrong,
I started getting better
at being right.

Let the word brave
be the hum on our lips
when we're afraid.
Let it become a song
so vibrant, so vocal
that it makes
others around us brave.
There is enough brave
to go around,
and if more people
did more brave things
like love
like accept
like listen
like hold hands
like speak out
we could create a world
that requires less bravery.

A radical theory:
What if we thanked our mess
if we thanked our addiction
if we thanked our depression
if we thanked our anxiety
if we thanked our rage
if we thanked our trauma
if we thanked our mess
then maybe
just as with a thank you note
we would be able to
put a stamp on it
and fondly let it go.

This much I know,
that to be deeply known
is one of the five loveliest things
in the world.
I'll let you know
when I find out
what the other four are.

A truly powerful woman
does not hoard her power,
she waters her sisters with it
so they can bloom too.
She is not threatened by
all they can do,
she is fed by it.

In connecting
with all versions of me:
I had ignored
young me for so long
that it wasn't until 26
that I gave her my heart
and she took it
and planted it
in the ground
and watered it
with tears and laughter
and put her arm
around my waist
so we could watch it
grow together.

And for my next trick
with a small turn of phrase
I will begin to change
shame into graciousness,
instead of, "I am inadequate"
or "I am a failure",
I will say, "I am learning".

A note to myself:
If he cannot be found
every now and again
with his nose in a book,
his nose doesn't belong
anywhere near you.

For a woman
to seek affirmation
or worthiness
from a man,
is like watering a flower
at its petals
not its roots.
It touches you
for a moment
then it runs off.
It won't nourish you.

If you try to fix people
you are implying
that they are broken.
If you try to love people
you are implying
that they are
worthy of love.

Grace isn't forget,
it's anyway.
It's not passive
it's purposeful.

Don't let anyone tell you
that you are only one thing.
Don't let that word
ring in your ears—
stupid, ugly, dramatic,
small, unworthy, powerless.
You are your unique laugh,
you are your favorite song,
you are a deep pool
of memory and thought,
you are the smile
on your best friend's face.
So much more
than one thing.

I am a lover
and a fighter.
There is no 'not' in me.
I feel deeply
and I also
push back at life.

In the small
or perhaps vast
collection of the people
that you love,
I hope that
you're among them.
There's nothing like
having coffee with yourself
and enjoying the company.

Do you know
those two minutes in the morning
as you're slowly opening your eyes?
Nothing is fast yet
before coffee
before the alarm
all is quiet?
There you show your character,
when you decide to be brave
in an unkind world
and put your feet on the floor.
You have been championing
these two minutes
your entire life;
keep it up.

All the tenderness
of a flower
without dying
in the frost.

I think God
painted us all
a little differently
because he loves
the beauty,
the art of color
of variety
of vibrancy.
There goes the world
once again
twisting something good,
something Godly.

And when I was determined
not to smile
you said,
"They don't make smiles
like yours anymore".
And I couldn't help myself.

I used to hear
all of their "can'ts"
when I would open my mouth
in intellectual conversations.
I could feel the inferiority
bubble up in my stomach.
But their "can'ts"
have now become kindling
and I am on fire
with all I can do,
all I can be.

I just want to grow
in every direction,
around any obstacle in my way.
Like when you see
a tree grow around
or through a fence.
I don't want anything
to stop me.

Should you ever
want to know
what a woman loves,
what a woman hopes,
what makes a woman laugh,
what makes her
get up in the morning,
look at her bookshelf.

I am my friends' laughter, even the snorts.
I am my grandmothers
pineapple upside down cake.
I am the little girl talking
to flowers and earthworms.
I am summer nights
catching lightening bugs
with my sister.
I am my dad's car windows down
singing to Billy Joel.
I am the winning shot that I made,
and the losing shot that I missed.
I am the music that makes it okay.
I am my mothers, "try again".
I am the smell of my books.
I am the reeds
on the beach of lake Michigan.
I am my dad carrying me inside
from a day at the beach.
I am the dirt
in my mother's flower bed.

I remember wondering
as a girl that,
if the sun is food for flowers
what is the moon to them?
I now know
that the moon
loves them when it is dark
and that is a beautiful, persistent
kind of love.

I believe that one day
reality will be so good
that I won't want to daydream,
I'll be living the daydream.

It is simply marvelous
how each of us
have made it through
every single day
of our lives.

The only negative thing
about poetry
is that you cannot
see the tender conviction
in my eyes
nor hear the strength
in my voice
when I say,
"to me, you're lovely".

I would rather
be called lovely
than beautiful.
If they call you beautiful
they are only saying
that you look gorgeous.
If they call you lovely
they are saying
you feel gorgeous.

She called me a quiet person,
and I was shocked.
It occurred to me
this is because
my mouth was closed.
But in my mind
I am always talking.
There is always
a vast array of daydreams,
conversations and questions,
thoughts and curiosities,
arguments and quirky quips,
words I've heard and read.
This can make for
quite a loud inner world.
This is why I chuckled
when she said she thought
I was a quiet person.

When I learned to say,
"yes" to the things
that water me,
that bring me sun,
and learn to unapologetically
say, "no"
to things that do not
belong in the garden,
therein lay my power.

I just want someone
to contradict me,
to correct me,
to fight with me
when I say I am
not good enough,
when I say that I am crazy,
when I plan for
disappointment or failure,
when I feel unlovable,
when I ask them
why they are with me.
I want him to be
confrontation dressed in tenderness.

I started healing
when I started speaking.
Both onto journal pages
and into the air.

Pretty often, I feel like
I need to know more
than I currently know
about life and things.
Then I remember
that I am 26-years-old
and today I know more
than I ever have,
and that's good enough.

I am becoming a woman
that I think
I could love.
And that my dears,
is revolutionary.

Golly.
I get it wrong so often.
This is how I've learned
that humility is never
a bad response
to a hard conversation.
I know because
I need it.
I need the mercy of humility.

I recently discovered
that I have a great
relationship with
my independence,
and a lot of love to give.
I also love myself
enough to know
that if I am going to
modify my independence
to open up this heart
and this mind,
I am going to need
a very good reason.

In learning to be okay about me:
She asked, "Yeah, but how
do you actually do that?"
I thought for a moment and said,
"I am not totally sure...
there was not a day
where I woke up and felt
remarkably different.
I just slowly noticed
the voice in my head
becoming kinder,
and I realized that
I am the only person
I get to be,
and if I can't be okay about that
I am going to spend my entire life
unsatisfied with something good.
I am the only real home
I will ever always have."

There are so many
people out there
smarter than me,
more successful than me,
more talented than me.
There, I said it.
I am disarmed.
And I can go on trying,
making mistakes,
putting the beauty
I have to offer
out into the world,
and forget about perfection.

There were so many times
when I was looking down
at my phone smiling,
and someone would walk up
and ask me what guy
has got me smiling.
I answered, it's my sister
who has got me smiling.
It is my best friend
who has got me smiling.
It is my godmother
who has got me smiling.
I had so many reasons to smile,
and not a single man.

Father, I'm so glad
I got to see you cry
when I was a little girl.
It taught me that
a man who weeps,
a man who feels,
does not have
to be a luxury.

I hunger for the day
we see another woman succeed
and feel not a single pang
of comparison, envy, or criticism.
But instead pride and victory
on her behalf.
Adding good is adding good,
who cares who it comes from.
This is the day we take flight.

All I is ask, is that you
read old books to me.
That we have picnics
and you call me lovely.
That you look at me often
as you looked at me at first.
That you tell me,
"I love you more
than this fight".
That we sit together
and do not have to talk.
That you express your emotions
and that I catch you smiling at me
when you thought
I wasn't looking.

Changing our questions:
Instead of is this the right path?
Ask, will I grow?
Instead of is this the right person?
Ask, can I breathe here?
Instead of what will happen?
Ask, what can I make happen?
Instead of will I ever be __?
Ask, how can I love
this perceived deficiency?
Instead of where should I go?
Ask, am I at home in me?
Instead of what can I get?
Ask, what can I create?

I don't want to fall in love,
I want to land in love
like a leaf in autumn.
Beautifully, naturally, softly.

I am so close
to settling
for less than
I deserve.
And now that
I see that line,
I am going to
take several
large steps back
and remember,
realize,
what I'm worth.

If you are different,
weird,
awkward,
strange,
in any way, thank you.
I say that
because I don't know
if anyone ever has.
We need you.
Dive into your differentness
and when you emerge
I swear you'll glow.
I stopped fighting
my differentness
when I realized
that others needed it.
We need yours too.

I wish I could remember
every face I've ever seen.
The lines
the creases
the iris'
the cheekbones.
Everyone deserves
to be seen.

I am so constantly impressed
by the wonder women
in my life.
They are brilliant and bright,
kind and true,
tender and strong.
I think about them,
and I could just burst
in fondness for them.

Try to remember
that a normal day
is actually good
is actually lovely
is actually miraculous.
We just get used to it
and rename it normal.
There is so much
miraculous we miss
by calling it normal.

For the most part,
I think people do
the things they do,
maladaptive or not,
because they think
it's their best shot
at being loved.
It may not look like it
but trace it back,
you'll see it.

I love that
I love a lot of people
who believe
very different things.
It would certainly
be more comfortable
if we all believed
the same things.
But comfortable
isn't colorful,
and I don't want
a bland world.
You don't learn
anything new
in an echo chamber.

I used to trade
my opinions in for silence.
I used to open my mouth
to speak,
and not hear any words
come out.
Because being loved
was more important
than the truth.
Then, I learned that
they are not
mutually exclusive.
In fact,
they need each other.

A sign of growth:
Things that used
to frighten me,
I now do daily.
When you do brave things
despite fear
you become a professor
on courage.
You know it well
you do it daily
and you can
show others the way.

I have always
been at home
in the water.
The fluid movement
like a dance
the weightlessness
the sensation on my skin
the refraction of the sun.
I always had to be
called out of it as a child.
I suppose it's because
it's the closest thing
I could find
to flying.

I had so many
good questions
as a little girl
that were shushed.
"He's sad, why doesn't he cry?"
"Why is pink a girl color?"
"Why do I have to sit still all the time?"
"How come boys are mean?"
"Why can't I fly, in the stories I write?"
"How come angry people
 don't talk to each other?"
It begs another question.
Why we listen to adults
more than children?

What a rare, gorgeous,
liberating, downright rebellious thing
to love who you are.
Not buts, ifs, coulds, shoulds, whens
just completely free of caveats.
Just completely okay about you.
I hope this feeling
finds you and me someday.

You do not know
the height
nor the depth
of my strength
until you've met
the powerful
tender
gorgeous
brilliant
women
that lift and carry me
when I fall,
and smile and cheer
when I rise.

When there was a warm spring rain
and I could hear the grass
thanking the sky for its greenness,
I would walk around clumsily
in my Gap overalls
and my light-up, untied shoes
and I would pick up earthworms
before the rain dried
and I would put them in the mud
because I thought
the world was better
with more living things.

Growth:
Before, if I had a garden
in it, I would grow love.
I would gather it up
in bunches
and I would give it all
away to others.
And now
should I have
the same garden
I would keep a little
for myself.

To me,
there is no greater compliment
than this,
"You're a safe person".
I wish that it weren't true
that humans
were the biggest threat
to humans.
Yet still, and rare,
there are safe ones.

Hold me accountable.
Hold me to a high standard.
Hold me to promises.
But mostly, just hold me.

Sometimes
less words
mean more,
than more words.
For example,
I could write you
a whole novel
to tell you that
I love you,
and it might be
romantic and all,
but I don't want you
to have to figure out
that I love you.
I want to say it.
I want it to be clear.

I'm going to go ahead
and argue that life,
in healing,
is about becoming and revealing.
For me, it was never about
becoming something new.
It has been about becoming and revealing
who I have always been,
this old soul,
and scraping away traces and residue
of the ugly parts of the world
that got on me
until I sparkle like new.

How beautiful is it
that in a relationship
it's another person job
to know you.

I've been thinking about
all of the threads I have been
hanging on by lately.
My sisters laugh,
repetitive whispers, "you can",
my grandfather's 94-year-old wisdom,
underrated sunshine,
pride in friends
taking flight in their lives,
Georgia's incredible blueberries right now.
For the first time,
in a long time,
there are a lot more than one.

You know how trees
produce oxygen?
I think the world
would be a much better place
if more of us
were like that.
I want to be like a tree.
But emit and radiate kindness,
to put good things
out into the world.

When I was a little girl
reading Where the Sidewalk Ends
by Shel Silverstein
and marveling at his
poignant truths and his silliness
awake at 3:00 am because
my Ritalin kept me from sleeping,
I didn't know that
in watching
and listening
and feeling
and noticing
and then putting words
in a specific, careful order
could make me a poet.

I can feel myself
becoming softer.
Things I would have
swallowed and held
in my chest,
made stern and hard my face,
hushed and coaxed
the tears back before
are pouring out
and somehow when
I look at my face
in the mirror
I look more like me
than I ever have.

For the first time
in a long time,
I can hear myself breathing.
And in between breaths
in those quiet moments
where my chest rises and falls,
I can feel the truth
coming out of my pores
coming out of my mouth
for the first time.
And it feels like light.

Who knew a person
could be alive for 26 years
before coming to life.
So this is breathing.

A WORD FROM THE AUTHOR

This year I was split open.
And I thought that if it was
going to hurt that bad,
something beautiful
might as well come out of it.
It brought me healing to write it,
I hope you feel some of that too.

7

Made in the USA
Columbia, SC
18 December 2019

85243702R00169